WHAT IS TH...

Written by Elena Martin
Illustrated by Kathryn Mitter

Harcourt Achieve
Rigby • Saxon • Steck-Vaughn

www.HarcourtAchieve.com
1.800.531.5015

Sue painted a picture.
Everyone called her an artist.

Jen painted a picture, too.
What could it be?

Sue thought it was a tree.

Dad thought it was a table.

Mom thought it was an elephant.

Arf! Arf! Arf! Coco barked.
What is it, Coco?

Jen smiled.
You are right, Coco!

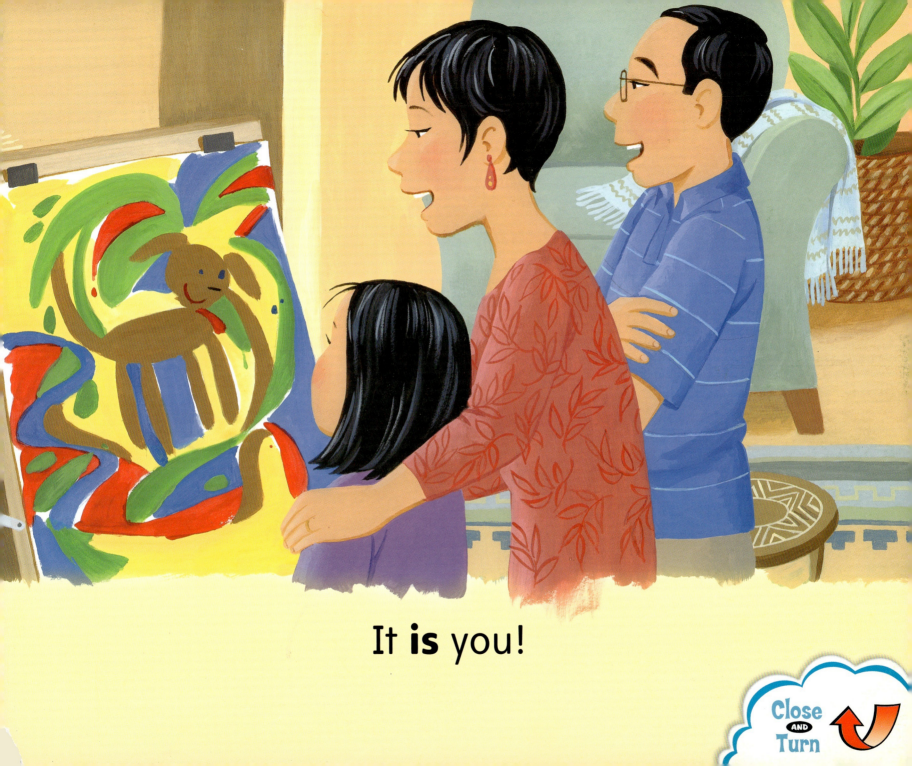

It **is** you!

There are many animals in the art we see!

An artist painted these birds in a tree.

An artist made this monkey small.

An artist drew this horse on a wall.

An artist painted this cat with care.

An artist made this mask to wear.

Animals in Art

Written by Elena Martin

Rigby • Saxon • Steck-Vaughn

www.HarcourtAchieve.com
1.800.531.5015